OTIS GROWS

By Kathryn Hast
Illustrated by L. M. Phang

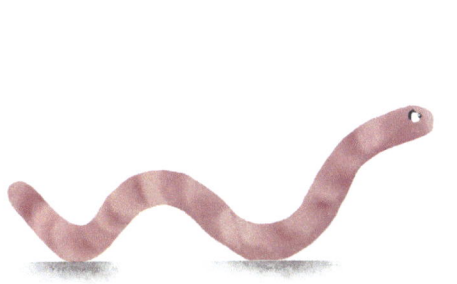

At the bottom of a hill,
not too far from you,
a small creek leaks past pebbles,
and sandy banks, too.
It babbles, and gurgles,
and trickles on through
a world that's too busy
with work, money, and school.

On each side of the creek,
there are groups, very small.
You must crouch down to see them;
you must slow to a crawl.
See there, the Yes-Chums live in the lull
by the yellow Nuh-Uhs.
The two groups tend to brawl.

When you lean a bit closer, the Nuh-Uhs look like chickens.
They have beaks, and gobblers, and webbed feet that they kick in.
When their feathers get ruffled, their heartbeats all quicken,
and they run in their circles, getting pushed and packed in.

Their wings flap like crazy as they squawk, peck, and shove,
and of course, what's worse: they wear big boxing gloves!
It's not that they're vicious; it's change that they love.
They want the world to be better. They try flying above.

It would seem the Yes-Chums are just some flowers:
their stalks are so soft, yet they manage to tower.
They cry, "**Yes, Chums!**" every hour on the hour.
And as time passes, they last with their pride and their power.

Their blue petals reach up to cup in the light,
and their roots, army boots, stomp down the dirt's fight.
They will not be soiled, won't give wrong the right.
They even grow in the snow. And they glow in the night.

So by the creek there they battle,
yellow and blue.
Both want what is right—
they want the other to lose.
But of course, with war's curse,
the inverse is true,
for when you fight for what's right,
what's right can fall through.

In the midst of this world,
this mad wonderland,
is a red onion named Otis,
who does not understand.
A proud, yellow Nuh-Uh
is his mother, and
his Yes-Chum dad says
the blue side is grand.

Pecking, his mom says he must flap, he must try.
"Plant your roots," nods his dad. And this also seems wise.
Otis, in the middle, feels the need to decide,
but as an onion, he's scared he'll just make them both cry.

He holds onto his skin,
though it wants to flake off.
It's now dry, aged, and brittle;
he no longer is soft.
In that creek, as a bulb,
he used to happily bob.
But floating is over.
When did it suddenly stop?

On one dreadful day, the fighting is bad.
From what Otis knows, it's the worst that they've had.
A blue petal-bomb falls, and as it goes *splat*,
the Yes-Chums seem so terribly glad.

The Nuh-Uhs, in response,
shed their feathers at once.
Enough is enough! They are sick of these stunts!
So feathers blind the Yes-Chums on all fronts,
but it's Otis, poor Otis, who feels the most punch.

Confused and sad,
he runs away from that place.
Up the bank, toward the tree:
all he wants is escape.
But as a big onion,
he can't keep a good pace.
Exhausted, he stops.
He hasn't even been chased.

He's breathing so hard, he's so red, he could scream,
"My dad's blue, my mom's yellow—I'm on nobody's team!"
Then suddenly, he sees a bright, beautiful gleam.
He rubs his eyes and blinks twice. He must be in a dream.

A skinny, clear rock walks toward him, aglow.
As the sunlight casts through her,
the rays turn to rainbows.
Smiling, she points to a nearby dirt road.
Otis thinks twice, but she says,

"Come, follow."

The road twists, and it turns, and Otis gets dizzy.
He sees colors: unclear, colliding, and busy.
At road's end, he's faced with a painting that's pretty.
"It's art," she explains. "The canvas of history."

"Wow," Otis mumbles.
"That sounds kind of cool."
"Yes," says Crystal,
"It's a great healing tool.
When people feel sad,
or when the world seems too cruel,
they can look here to see
all that's been beautiful."

"And here where there's need, there's Teresa, a nun. She blesses poor children in the heat of the sun."

"Then quietly sitting amidst hate is Nelson, who, through peace, calls for love and freedom..."

"Wow!" Otis cries. "All this happens right here?
In the world right around us—right here, in the clear?"

Crystal smiles and says, "Yes, my dear,
It's lovely, but wait. There's more you should hear."

Too late. He is gone.
He's run back to that creek.
He is thrilled! So excited,
he can't even speak.
He will find his parents and simply repeat
how the world is not angry,
but loving and sweet.

Otis sees his dad first
at the end of the road.
From a distance, it's weird:
he somehow seems old.
Still, Otis tells all there is to be told
with the hope this perspective
could help break the mold.

His dad simply nods,
as if he always was sure.
"Yes, Chum!" he replies,
"They're the folks we prefer.
Growing up they looked out
with purpose and thirst,
and did all they could do
to make their dream work."

"Nuh-uh!"

cries his mom, who has flown in, quite mad.
"The famous and powerful always say that!
It is not so easy to be head of the pack.
In fact, it is better to resist all that flack."

"This just figures!" his dad yells, "Your son is done for!"
"Could be," shouts his mom, "If he buys your folklore!"
Still screaming, they make their way back to their shores.
They don't notice Otis. They know only their war.

Had they been listening and not looking to win,
they would have seen that their son shed a layer of skin.
Now with tears filling his eyes to the brim,
he fights the odor of growing older
that comes from within.

But then he hears her calling.
"Otis, come back!"
Sure enough, there is Crystal
walking back down the path.

"You can simply resist all this anger and wrath.
Just know that you're both your mom and your dad."

He asks, "How can that be?"
And then he grows tall.
"What's happening to me?
It feels like I could fall!"

Next--*pop*!
Wings sprout without any flaw.
Otis flaps, distracted
by the sound of applause.

From this new view he sees them,
clapping for him.
His mom's gloves are off;
his dad's boots are limp.
They both gaze and grin,
as if he were the gem.
"Crystal," he says,
"Wow. Look at them."

"Well, of course!" she exclaims,
what a marvel you are!"
"Are you making fun of me?"
He flaps. "I've done you no harm…"
"But I'm not making fun.
Look how you move, what a star!
You have music and rhythm
—you're bound to go far!"

"See, there are folks who will shine, who will crackle and spark, and there are those vying to find sense in the dark. In between these extremes, you must make your mark as someone who grows without losing his heart."

So Otis grows.
It begins to make sense.
There's a world beyond this creek,
and that world is immense.
With some self-direction
and a whole lot of chance
He will find ways to be
like both of his parents.

Too often we rush past creeks like these.
We don't hear the ripple; we don't feel the breeze.
We don't stop to recall our own questions and needs;
We ignore our own Otis, there in the weeds.

So remember that creek, the red, yellow and blue,
for all of those colors are somewhere in you.
Because of conflict and wonder, like Otis, you grew,
and will continue to grow,

because that's what we do.

www.ingramcontent.com/pod-product-compliance
Lightning Source LLC
Chambersburg PA
CBHW040729150426
42811CB00063B/1542